NATURAL
LIVING style

Selina Lake
NATURAL LIVING style

INSPIRATIONAL IDEAS
FOR A BEAUTIFUL &
SUSTAINABLE HOME

PHOTOGRAPHY BY RACHEL WHITING

RYLAND PETERS & SMALL
LONDON • NEW YORK

Senior designer Megan Smith
Senior commissioning editor
Annabel Morgan
Location research Jess Walton
Production manager
Gordana Simakovic
Art director Leslie Harrington
Editorial director Julia Charles
Publisher Cindy Richards

First published in 2019 by
Ryland Peters & Small
20–21 Jockey's Fields
London WC1R 4BW
and
341 E 116th Street
New York, NY 10029

www.rylandpeters.com

Text copyright © Selina Lake 2019
Design and photographs copyright
© Ryland Peters & Small 2019

10 9 8 7 6 5 4 3 2 1

ISBN 978-1-78879-066-6

A CIP record for this book is available
from the British Library.

Library of Congress CIP data has been
applied for.

Printed and bound in China

MIX
Paper from
responsible sources
FSC® C106563
www.fsc.org

contents

introduction

Currently the issue of protecting our planet is a hot topic, constantly discussed by the world's media, politicians and environmentalists along with individuals trying to make a difference, while the legend that is Sir David Attenborough has highlighted the plastic filling our oceans in his BBC TV programmes.

As I become increasingly aware of these issues, I look back at all the plastics that have come and gone in my life. I feel guilty about the cartoon-character plastic lunchbox that I took to junior school and can't help but wonder where it is now. Experts predict that plastic will take up to 1,000 years to break down and in the process will release tiny particles of plastic into streams, rivers and the ocean, causing harm to animals, the environment and us. And plastic is just one concern. There are many threats to our planet – global warming, pollution, overpopulation and water scarcity – and it's easy to feel powerless in the face of all this bad news. As a stylist, I wondered how we can make our homes, work spaces and gardens more in harmony with the environment while keeping them beautiful? Can a stylish, comfortable, efficient home be achieved with minimal impact on the environment?

For those of you who are concerned about the subject, I have put together this book to share my ideas for making your home more sustainable and eco friendly as well as aesthetically pleasing and practical. I hope I can inspire you to approach your home environment in a different way. We can all do our bit for the planet and, in turn, benefit from a home that is as chemical and waste free as possible.

I've come to the conclusion that everything turns full circle – fashion trends, the way we live, the food we eat and so on. Even though technology and other modern developments have provided us in the West with everything we need on tap, or at the touch of a smart phone or tablet, the irony is that we are constantly striving for what our grandparents saw as the norm – a simple, comfortable, Natural Living Style.

Need inspiration for stylish ways to go plastic free and to decorate your home in a more sustainable, eco-friendly way? Throughout this book, I have explored gorgeous organic gardens, eco retreats and homes to find the best Natural Living ideas to share with you. As well as zero-waste solutions, look out for simple craft projects and styling tips.

NATURAL
inspirations

living a greener life

When environmental issues impact upon our style choices, the results can only mean a more efficient, natural home and garden. Going green and quitting the use of plastics (especially single-use plastics) go hand in hand, but this is not made easy for us, with manufacturers and supermarkets selling pretty much all their products covered, shrinkwrapped or packed in the stuff. Giving up plastic can be hard. If you've ever attempted to give up sugar, you'll know that you keep finding it hidden in everything, and it's the same with plastic – you can't get away from it. Even eco cleaning sprays are sold in plastic bottles and many tea bags are sealed with polypropylene.

To make your home greener, the first step is to produce less waste. This means buying less, making full use of items you already own, borrowing and lending from/to family or neighbours and fixing anything in need of repair. The next goal is to recycle. Create an efficient system that works both for your home and your community's recycling initiatives. Recycling bins can clutter the

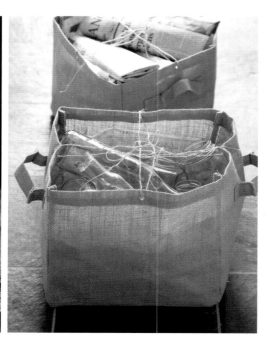

MADE TO LAST
Most of the wood used for the flooring and to clad the walls at the Lindeborgs Eco Retreat in Nyköping, Sweden, comes directly from their own forest. The stylish ash table is by Melo Studio, and the chairs are Sami Kallio for &Tradition (opposite). Beechwood egg cups are a lovely way to serve boiled eggs (above left) and the classic Falcon Enamelware teapot (above centre) is pretty much indestructible, making it a kitchen essential. These sturdy hemp bags make practical receptacles for the household recycling (above right).

SHOP LOCAL

I find farm shops inspiring – it's such a treat to buy fresh produce direct from growers and farmers (this page and opposite below right). This way of shopping used to be the norm before supermarket chains took over. If you live in a city, find out if there's a farmers' market nearby, or look online for city community farms and gardens that offer produce for sale. Farm shops often collaborate with local artists and designers and sell their wares alongside fruit, flowers and vegetables – next time you visit such a place, look out for homeware items for your Natural Living Style home.

BRING A BOTTLE
When I was little, milk was delivered by the milkman in glass bottles that, after use, were collected, washed and reused. Then supermarket chains started to sell milk cheaply in plastic bottles, which had a huge effect both on farmers and the environment. In recent years, milk delivery services have become popular again, thanks to demands for fairer milk prices for farmers and recyclable glass bottles plus the convenience of having milk delivered to the door (left).

kitchen, so choose containers that look good. I have used hemp bags to hold our glass and paper for recycling for many years.

Next, become a savvy consumer. In our homes, the materials we choose to decorate with are not only key to the overall style but also have an effect on the environment. Opting for eco-friendly items will put less strain on the planet. Use recycled or reclaimed wood, such as salvaged floorboards, to clad internal walls for decoration, and find new uses for things that might otherwise end up in landfill. If you are buying new items, try to choose products made from sustainable materials. If, like me, you are consciously trying to reduce your environmental footprint, hunt out natural alternatives for home accessories, such as organic cotton bedding, sustainable natural fibre flooring and paints that contain fewer harmful chemicals, Farrow & Ball do a range of water-based, low-VOC (volatile organic compounds) paints that are eco friendly and kinder to the environment.

HOMEMADE HOMES

Throughout this book, I have explored homes designed by owners who have been mindful of the materials they choose for their interior and exterior design projects. From wood-clad walls and virtually plastic-free kitchens to extensions/ additions built using salvaged items, these spaces are filled with handmade details, like these sofa cushions made from vintage Liberty fabrics (right) and the artisan ceramics decorating these kitchen shelves (opposite).

TAKE IT SLOW
*Don't rush redecoration –
take time to research green
materials. This gorgeous
kitchen is in the summerhouse
of garden designer Dorthe
Kvist. It's a work in progress
– the plywood panels look
great, but they are actually
a base that handmade tiles
will be laid upon.*

NATURAL
ingredients

MATERIALS
for natural living

Explore natural materials and items made from natural fibres such as seagrass, rattan and coir when furnishing your home and garden. Introducing found elements will give your space a natural, organic feel.

When creating a living space, the materials we choose to furnish and decorate it with are not only key to the overall style but, of course, will also have an impact on the environment. Opting for items made from sustainable, ethically made and environmentally benign materials will put less strain on the planet. We are all aware of the damaging effects of excess plastic consumption, climate change, deforestation and pollution, and know that it makes sense to choose eco-friendly alternatives wherever possible. Environmental issues are currently at the forefront of

people's minds and it's not just a trend – it's becoming something of a movement. I want to live in a lovely home, but I also want to be a conscious consumer and to source furnishings that are ethically produced with less or little impact on the environment. I'm also trying to produce less waste by reducing what I consume, reusing whatever I can and sending as little as possible to landfill. This chapter is all about which materials to choose for natural and environmentally friendly living, and how to style them within different areas of your home.

RAW GOOD LOOKS
A stack of woven palm-leaf baskets with leather handles makes for stylish storage, laundry and grocery shopping (above left). Choose undyed linen and blankets made from organic wool (above centre). With their aged patina, wooden chopping boards look good and work hard in the kitchen (above right). Rattan lampshades of various shapes and sizes hang in a cabin at The Norrmans B&B in Denmark (opposite).

RECYCLABLE MATERIALS
wood, glass & metal

Wood is a sustainable material but can't be easily recycled, which is why it's important to reuse wooden objects until they become rickety or fall apart (at which point they can be moved outside to biodegrade). It is renewable, but deforestation is a huge environmental issue, so if you are buying new wood, look for FSC (Forest Stewardship Council)-certified wood to protect the world's forests. Glass is made from all-natural, sustainable raw materials. It is 100% recyclable and can be recycled endlessly without any loss in quality. It can also be reused in the home – just wash out food jars and repurpose them for storing dry goods or toiletries. Metal is a desirable and valuable material that, like glass, can be recycled repeatedly without altering its properties. It requires much less energy to recycle metal than it does to extract it in the first place, so it's important to recycle all food and drink containers made from aluminium or steel. As it's strong and durable, metal components can also be salvaged and reused in the home – think of old sewing machine tables with decorative trestles or planters made from traditional metal dolly tubs and buckets.

Take inspiration from the LA-EVA studio in Oxfordshire, where the work table is made from two log trestles with a top fashioned from recycled wooden boards (opposite). Recycled metal vessels make great garden planters (above left). A handcrafted vase made from recycled glass has a lovely rustic finish and organic form (above).

ALL NATURAL

Handmade woven palm-leaf wall hangings from Danish brand Madam Stoltz provide an appealing backdrop for this attractive timeworn table and chair set (above). Recycled glass bottles used as bud vases for single stems make for a simple, pared-back display (above left). Handcrafted items tend to have a raw and honest appeal, like this collection of rustic wooden spoons (left).

ZERO WASTE
Making use of old furniture is an excellent way to be waste free. This vintage pine kitchen table warms up a minimalist interior and will last several lifetimes!

GALVANIZE YOURSELF
Galvanized steel buckets and containers are my go-to vessels for planters. Galvanizing is a process by which zinc is applied to iron or steel to prevent rusting. Steel is one of the easiest materials to recycle, making it a very energy-efficient metal. Even better, galvanized items age attractively, developing a rich patina with freckles of rust.

ECO-FRIENDLY MATERIALS
bamboo, cork, sisal & rattan

Fibres harvested from trees, plants and shrubs are among the most sustainable and eco-friendly materials available. Bamboo canes are strong and abundant, rattan comes from a naturally renewable palm and fibres from the agave plant are turned into strong sisal for baskets, rugs and carpets. Bamboo cane furniture like that shown opposite was all the rage in the 1970s and has made a comeback in recent years. It's a hardwearing material, so ideal for furniture and a good replacement for plastic. Look out for second-hand bamboo furniture – items can be given a new life in your home or garden. Cork is harvested from the bark of the cork oak tree and is buoyant, waterproof and flexible – also a brilliant substitute for plastic. Often used in the fabric of a building for insulation, it has a lovely dappled finish, making it a good choice for wall cladding, furniture and tableware. Its amazing properties of insulation prevent heat loss so it is a very green material.

FAIR TRADE
In beautiful natural seagrass, this placemat was handmade by talented artisans in Vietnam and is available via Also Home. The organic look and feel of the natural material brings a laid-back and relaxed setting to your table (above left). Handwoven in Morocco, this cute mini basket is made from palm leaves and is an eco-friendly alternative to plastic containers (above centre). These ethical and fair-trade sisal baskets, handmade in Africa and sold via The Basket Room, make gorgeous storage containers (above right).

INTERESTING TEXTURES
Cork insulation used as a wall covering makes a style statement in the reception at The Norrmans B&B in Denmark (this page). A rattan and bamboo screen provides privacy in an outdoor shower area that offers an instant connection with nature (opposite).

Moroccan-style tadelakt plaster creates a textural backdrop in this hallway (opposite). Interior designer Beth Dadswell used a limited palette of materials including brass, plaster and concrete plus eco-friendly paint to put an elegant twist on industrial style for her hallway in South London (above left). Original cupboards in a Dutch home have been painted Light Blue by Farrow & Ball (above).

ECO-FRIENDLY MATERIALS
paint & lime plaster

Natural walls have a subtle finish that brings warmth to any room. One eco-friendly wall treatment is tadelakt, a traditional Moroccan surfacing technique that can be used to create bathtubs, sinks, walls, ceilings and even floors. It is made from lime plaster, which is polished, then treated with soap to make it waterproof and create a lustrous, seamless finish. Raw plaster walls are a current trend – avoid gypsum plaster or cement and go for breathable eco plaster for a green alternative that naturally regulates moisture in the home. Bauwerk is a paint company producing lime paint made from clay, minerals and natural pigments. It has a beautiful, understated finish and doesn't give off toxic fumes. Farrow & Ball are another of my go-to paint suppliers – they produce water-based, low-VOC paints in a range of hard-to-choose-between colours.

Natural textiles from ScandaloAlSole via Etsy (above). Their products includes raw linen napkins and tablecloths and hemp home accessories. This nomadic-style nook in the LA-EVA studio is a visual feast of antique kilims and throws sourced by Louisa Maybury (left). A Communauté de biens turmeric linen cushion from Smallable adds a pop of colour to a wood-clad bedroom (opposite).

NATURAL FIBRES
organic cotton, linen & wool

Textiles are an easy way to update a room – rugs, curtains, flooring, bedding and soft furnishings can all be swapped and moved round for a fresh look. When looking for textiles, try to choose those that have the smallest environmental footprint, such as wool, which is renewable, biodegradable, recyclable and can be organically produced. Cotton and linen share some of these attributes, but traditional methods of cotton production use a huge amount of water, pesticides and chemicals. Look for GOTS (Global Organic Textile Standard)-certified organic cotton wherever possible. Linen is greener, as the flax plant is immune to pests and disease so doesn't require many chemical treatments when growing. Silk is natural and renewable, but needs a lot of mulberry leaves to feed the larvae that produce the thread. Other eco fabrics to look out for include bamboo, lyocell, made from wood pulp, and hemp, which can be grown without chemicals and creates a strong, sturdy material that's perfect for upholstery fabric, as it's so durable and takes dye well.

STYLE TIP

Instead of turning the heating up, layer up when it's chilly. Dress your bed with duvets, wool blankets and throws. Here, a linen tablecloth has been used as a bedspread rather than leaving it languishing in a drawer!

TACTILE TEXTILES

Give your living room a tranquil, sophisticated feel with elegant sofas covered in dark linen (opposite). Hemp upholstery fabric looks very similar to linen and is even more durable. Layering a bed with natural fibres strikes a cosy note in a minimalist sleeping space (above). Linen curtains look softer than wardrobe/closet doors in a bedroom (above right). Hang an old tablecloth from tension wire for an easy no-sew solution. Vintage fabrics found at fairs and car boot/yard sales can be made into napkins, cushions or drawstring bags. (right).

REUSE & UPCYCLE
for natural living

Reusing and repurposing items saves you money and saves them from landfill. They can also make a style statement. Look out too for companies making products from recycled plastics, rubber and other materials.

Large amounts of natural resources and energy have already been expended on manufacturing existing furniture and household items, so it makes sense to use, reuse and repurpose what we already have as much as possible. There are many companies who see waste as an exciting resource and are actively seeking ways to use recycled materials in their products. Weez & Merl in Brighton, UK, are exploring used plastics and making marbled tableware and furniture. Weaver Green have recycled 68 million plastic bottles and turned them into super-soft and tactile cushions and throws, and UK bed manufacturer Silentnight is pioneering a mattress filling made from recycled plastic bottles. I've even heard of a company called MacRebur that is making road surfacing from discarded plastic bags – and apparently it lasts even longer than tarmac. With all the bad press plastic is getting, it's tempting to throw out the plastic you own and replace it with eco-friendly alternatives. In fact this goes against zero-waste principles, so I'm trying to get as much use as possible out of my existing plastic, then repurposing it elsewhere in the home if I can.

WASTE NOT WANT NOT
Shelving made from scaffolding planks provides valuable storage space in this converted glasshouse (above left). Recreate this effect using a tin can as a vase for home-grown flowers (above centre). Old window frames with the original glass panes bring interest to a newly built summerhouse in Denmark (above right). An aged wooden trough on a wooden base has been repurposed as a sink in the LA-EVA studio (opposite).

furniture & storage

I keep talking about buying second-hand, vintage and salvaged items when possible because it makes more sense to reuse what's already here rather than throwing it in landfill and producing new stuff. Opting for antique and vintage furniture is a zero-waste, green choice. Older pieces also tend to be better quality and were made to last, unlike many of the mass-produced designs on offer in our throwaway society. And buying antique, vintage or preloved furniture is often cheaper, benefitting both the planet and our wallets. Retro furniture, especially that made in the 1960s, is very on-trend. Look for mid-century-style armchairs, sideboards and tables at car boot/yard sales and vintage fairs – such items are often neat in size and shape, making them perfect for modern homes. When it comes to new furniture, seek out eco brands. Ask questions about the company's environmental stance and whether the wood they use is FSC-certified. Remember that much cheap furniture is made using toxic chemicals such as formaldehyde – antiques are good for the planet and can be better for your health too!

The roughly plastered and limewashed walls and exposed window lintels offer the perfect contrast to a smart retro butterfly chair with a glossy leather finish (opposite). This industrial shelf unit came from Baileys Home (above left and right). With its sturdy metal frame and raw wooden shelves, it provides attractive storage.

STORE IT

Old wooden crates are a neat and tidy storage solution – the slatted sides make them breathable and they are designed to be stackable (right). Small sets of drawers can be displayed in the home office or hallway and used to hold post, keys, stationery or craft supplies (below). A natural rattan log basket completes a cosy fireside scene in this country cottage (bottom).

 MAKE *a shelving unit from reclaimed doors*

Can't find a rustic shelving unit? Try making one yourself. You will need a reclaimed wooden door from a local reclamation yard plus narrow planks, old shelves or pieces of wood, an electric saw, a power screwdriver, assorted screws and a spirit level (borrow or hire equipment if possible). The door you have sourced will dictate the size of the finished unit. Place the door face down and screw a couple of cross braces to the back to reinforce the structure. Now use the spirit level, screws and screwdriver to attach a base and top, then the sides. Add shelves as desired, using the spirit level to ensure they are straight.

FOUND OBJECTS

These old bricks were found on a beach in Greece (left). The salty seawater has eroded them slightly, giving them a smooth outline and rendering them very tactile. The bricks make great vases, as they have holes that can be lined with plastic bags (a good way to reuse them) to make them watertight. These sturdy plant stands have been built from recycled wood and make an attractive feature with scented pelargoniums in galvanized metal tubs placed on top (below).

 MAKE an outdoor sofa & table from old pallets

Making a pallet sofa is all about stacking! Collect used wood pallets (try and pick ones that are similar sizes), then give them all a coat of black exterior wood stain or paint, making sure you choose an eco-friendly option such as AURO. Once dry, prop two or three pallets in a row up against a garden wall on an even, level surface to make the back of the sofa. Now stack double layers of pallets in front to create the seat. For comfort, layer cushions along the wall and upon the seat base. The whole thing can be quickly and easily dismantled at the end of the summer.

Embarking on a property restoration? Save as many architectural details as possible while still meeting building regulations. Old mirrors can be reused in the garden if they don't fit the new space, while tables can be made from old doors. Create a garden like this by sourcing vintage dolly tubs to grow plants in – old ones are quite hard to find now and a little pricey, but worth it in order to complete the salvage look (left).

architectural salvage

I love the history behind this East London courtyard garden – the space was once a Victorian dairy and has been converted by designers Beth and Andrew into a family home. The couple were keen to salvage as many architectural details as possible from the old dairy, such as the glazed doors that have been repurposed as a divider between the off-street car parking space and their alfresco dining area (opposite). The legs of the garden table were bought from a dealer in architectural salvage and support a tabletop that's an old door rescued from the property. The old metal roof structure of the former dairy was retained and makes a striking feature overhead. Amazingly, all the plants, trees and shrubs in this garden are growing in pots and are positively thriving. Salvage yards and reclamation dealers are the best places to find interesting objects rescued from defunct buildings that you can incorporate into your own designs at home and in the garden.

ZERO WASTE

Andrew saw an opportunity to reuse the metal guttering beams from the old dairy to make the long light fittings that are suspended over the courtyard garden.

DECORATIVE DETAILS
for natural living

*It's the finishing touches that often make the most impact in a space.
Choose eco-friendly decorative items such as houseplants, vintage finds
and inherited accessories, and the result will be naturally beautiful.*

Adding decorative touches to rooms, such as art, flowers, candles and found objects, really brings the owner's personality to the fore. It gives a sense of a much-loved home where someone has taken time and effort to create a pleasing space for people to enjoy. It's a form of self-care, really! The possibilities for natural pretties are almost endless and many things can be sourced without spending any money. A single fallen branch gathered on a woodland walk can be placed in a vase creating a sculptural effect, while houseplants can be propagated. You and the kids can get creative to adorn your walls – children's artworks can look fabulous when framed. We all want to keep things out of landfill, so look out for hand-me-downs and inherited pieces – that 1950s mirror from a great aunt could add vintage charm to a modern bathroom. If you invest in new decorative pieces, support independent makers and look out for handmade items at craft fairs and events. Styling a table for a meal? Line a collection of scented soy candles in glass jars along the table and intertwine foliage and flowers in between – simple but effective.

PRETTY NATURAL
Nature is an abundant source of decorative inspiration. Flowers from a Swedish garden add botanical style to a table dotted with soy candles (above left). Flower heads in dainty bud vases look charming on an old metal plate (centre). These intricate birds' nests were found after nesting season when hedges were being trimmed (above right). Decorative details sit alongside each other on top of built-in storage (opposite).

display

For Natural Living Style displays, bring the outside in. Supermarket flowers flown halfway around the globe are not necessary. Instead, arrange bare branches in an old jug/pitcher on a sideboard or dresser/hutch place acorns or conkers in a ceramic bowl and display houseplants in woven baskets.

Collections of favourite natural items will give your room personality when they are put on display. Glazed cabinets with open shelves like the one shown (above right) are excellent options for displaying glass or ceramics. I am drawn to bare walls, especially if they have a lovely plaster or wood finish, but sometimes just one intriguing decorative object adds character to

a space as well as a connection with the natural world. If you're looking for artworks, Etsy is a good place to start, as many makers and designers sell handcrafted wares through the site. The screen-printed botanical wall hanging (above left) was designed and made by Aimee Mac Illustration and softens a dark wood-clad wall. Straw hats have the power to evoke summer days, lavender fields and country bike rides...or is that just me? I like the idea of using them as a wall display and it doubles up as storage. Other ideas for display pieces include cut branches after a garden clear-up, tree seeds like acorns and conkers, discarded feathers and dried flower heads such as hydrangeas.

TEXTURAL TREASURES

I used to love beachcombing, looking for a perfect shell or interesting stone to bring back from holiday. Nowadays, we know that taking shells or pebbles from beaches can damage coastal ecosystems, just as uprooting wild flowers can destroy the countryside. If you have a passion for coastal treasures, eco-friendly resin coral and shells look amazingly lifelike (above left). Feathers are a great way to bring the natural world indoors and can be arranged in ceramic or stone vases as an alternative to a flower arrangement (above). Dried seeds have intriguing shapes and textures – I display them in a shallow dish (left).

STYLE TIP
Give your art collection a
'green-over' – seek out vintage
art that might otherwise end up
in landfill. Pretty floral paintings
look lovely unframed and add
interest to a neutral backdrop.
Look for something similar
on eBay or Etsy.

MAKE a linen shopper

Start by cutting a length of linen fabric
(I used Iona linen by James Hare) into
two equal-sized rectangles. Using a sewing
machine, hem the top edge of each rectangle,
then place them right sides together and
stitch along the sides and bottom, leaving the
hemmed edge open. Cut two strips of fabric,
then fold and hem them to make straps. Stitch
the ends inside the opening on each side.

plants & flowers

It's always such a treat to display flowers and plants at home – they cheer up a dull space as well as putting a smile on your face. No one can have missed the huge boom in popularity of houseplants in recent years. Our Instagram feeds are awash with snaps of 'indoor jungles' and my previous book, *Botanical Style*, was an instant best-seller soon after release. Plants help strengthen our connection with nature. They also have therapeutic qualities and help to absorb carbon dioxide and other pollutants like carbon monoxide and formaldehyde, making for a healthier atmosphere. Scented flowers such as sweet peas, lilacs, mock orange and roses will perfume your space with seasonal scents too. Look out for unusual vessels for flowers – old lab jars and shot glasses for smaller sprigs and buds, and stoneware or glass vases for larger arrangements can all be found at flea markets, car boot/yard sales and in charity/thrift shops. Any chips, dents or scratches just add character! I am a firm believer that buying local or growing your own flowers is the best option, so head to pages 150-153 for tips on sourcing organic and locally grown flowers.

Natural tones and textures (above left and right). Privet cuttings are arranged in a stoneware vase (opposite top left). Assorted vases mixed with metal and rattan give this vignette Natural Living Style (opposite top right) Pilea peperomioides, *or Chinese money plant, brings botanical style to a simple shelf (opposite below left). Home-grown flowers work well against Farrow & Ball painted cupboards (opposite below right).*

BRING NATURE IN

Potted plants make gorgeous natural table decorations. To create a living screen like this one (opposite), hang up a row of pots of trailing ivy in macramé holders. English ivy, or Hedera helix, is a popular houseplant that not only looks great but also helps filter airborne toxins inside your home.

ZERO WASTE

Grow microgreens in pots made from plastic bottles. Line the bases with damp newspaper, then scatter seeds over it. Pop on a windowsill, water and watch them grow!

MAKE *a watering can from a plastic bottle*

This is a good way to reuse a plastic bottle with a handle and screw lid (above). Pierce the lid with a small screwdriver to make holes to allow the water to spray out. Use a permanent marker pen to draw a botanical decoration onto the bottle – do a freehand design or copy something from a book – then add sticker letters to spell out relevant words such as 'bloom' and 'grow'.

lighting

When I was a teenager, my dad was forever telling my sister and me to turn off the lights when we left a room. At the time, we thought he was nagging, but nowadays I'm equally concerned about wasting electricity! While lighting has the power to affect the mood and the functionality of our homes, it can also have a big effect on the planet. Traditional incandescent bulbs convert less than 5% of the energy they use into light, but luckily we now have LED (light-emitting diode) lamps, which can reduce energy consumption by 80–90%. When they were first available, the light produced was cool and harsh and the bulbs took a while to light up. Now they work much better and are available in warmer tones. With the resurgence in popularity of vintage Edison-style bulbs, lighting manufacturers have even developed energy-efficient LED alternatives to meet this trend. Eco-friendly shades are also important – look for lamps made from sustainable, natural and recyclable materials. Think about fittings too. When it comes to switches, for example, plastic versions are cheaper than metal ones but won't look as good or be as easily recyclable.

HANGING OUT
Delicate Chinese paper lanterns sourced from a flea market hang over the reception desk at The Norrmans B&B in Denmark (above left). The glass pendant above the dining table at the Lindeborgs Eco Retreat in Sweden is handcrafted from clear glass and raw brass, and holds an eco friendly LED Edison-style bulb (above centre). A vintage chandelier from antiques shop Martha's Attic sparkles in the LA-EVA studio in Oxfordshire, UK (above right). If you want truly green lighting, use soy or beeswax candles (opposite).

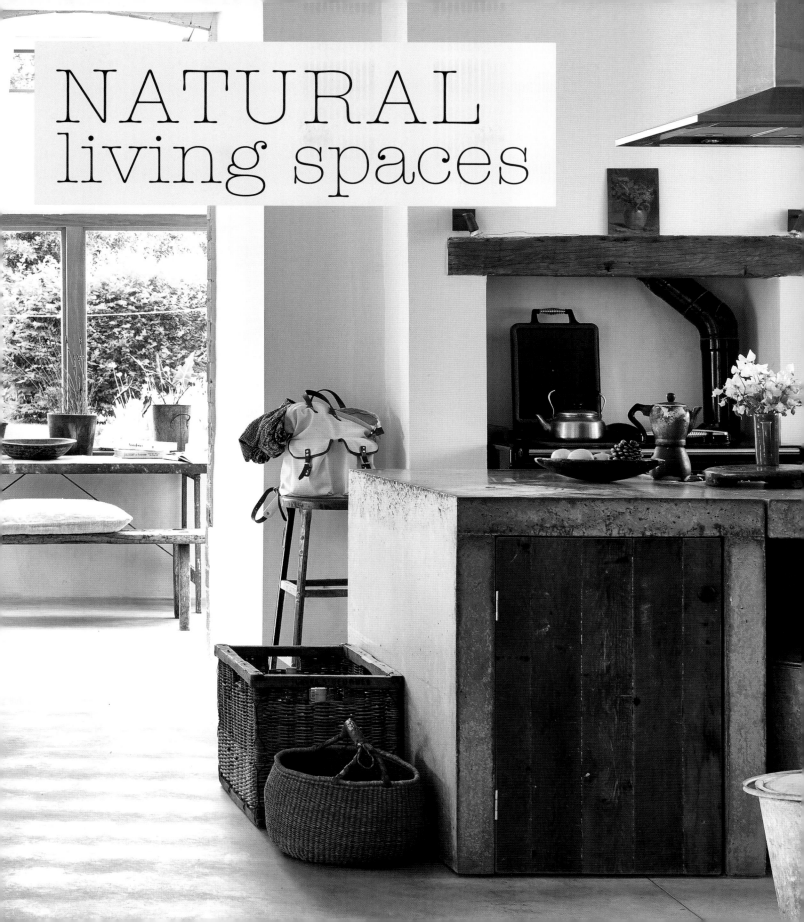

NATURAL
living spaces

LIVING
& relaxing

inside/outside living

Use plants to blur the divide between indoors and out.

Our living spaces are our havens, places for relaxation, enjoyment and family time, relaxing on comfy sofas and favourite armchairs. If you want your space to feel harmonious and calm, take inspiration from the home of interior designer Beth and her husband Andrew. They have introduced lots of natural elements into their home, which was once a derelict Victorian dairy, in a sought-after part of London. The couple have completely renovated the building and transformed it into a stunning home. After an environmentally friendly damp-proof course had been installed, all the walls were finished in eco-friendly lime plaster, which allows a building to breathe. The floors have been softened with natural seagrass rugs, while the black steel-framed windows and doors, with their industrial vibe, are double glazed with insulated frames that retain heat during the winter months and allow stunning views of the courtyard garden. The couple have mirrored the leafy view outside with an array of houseplants inside, which not only look good but will also eliminate pollutants from the air.

These black steel-framed windows and doors were made by Fabco Sanctuary; double glazed with insulated frames, they have a high thermal energy rating and span the front of the downstairs of the building. Interior designer Beth has used built-in storage to display the couple's collection of art, propping it against the lime-plastered walls.

BOTANICAL STYLE

Beth and Andrew's luscious courtyard garden was inspired by Parisian gardens and the shrubs, trees and plants are planted in pots, making for a movable display. Try to source plants from local independent nurseries if possible. The huge expanse of glass between inside and out is broken up with the black steel frames. If you aren't lucky enough to have such an appealing view, try suspending hanging houseplants in front of your window for a similar effect.

converted home

From Dutch auction house to natural family home.

It's hard to believe that this tranquil family home was once a busy auction house. Owners Miriam and Bas bought the property 15 years ago and with the help of Bas's brother, who is an architect, transformed the space into a home for their brood of seven. Miriam has two businesses, felt making and flower growing, and her creativity is evident throughout the interior. When tackling a conversion or makeover, the first step is to assess what you already have before rushing to invest in new things. Miriam inherited beautiful beamed ceilings and these have been painted a soft sage green using eco-friendly paint. Most of the furniture here is second hand – sourced at flea markets and junk shops or inherited. Old pieces were made to last, unlike many items produced today. The sofa, however, is a new purchase – one much needed for their large family. When it comes to buying new furniture, seek out eco-friendly brands. Enquire about the company's environmental stance and the provenance of their raw materials. Ask how items will be delivered to you, and if the packaging can be recycled once you have finished with it.

Miriam's home-grown poppies, earthenware vases and salt-glazed pottery make a pretty display on her wooden coffee table (above left and opposite). More flowers and plants in terracotta pots are scattered on available surfaces, while second-hand furniture has either been painted for a new look or left in its natural state (above).

STYLE TIP
Introduce natural details
to enhance your space:
a collection of botanical prints
grouped together in black-
stained wooden frames brings
interest to a bare wall, while
fresh flowers bring
a room to life.

ROADSIDE FINDS

These retro bamboo armchairs were found by the roadside and have been given a new life in the living and dining area. Miriam's handmade felt cushions and knitted wool throw add a homely touch to the modular sofa.

ZERO WASTE

All the furniture here was purchased second hand or from makers using reclaimed wood. The salvaged glass doors were bought at auction and bring light into this end of the building.

Recycled glass bottles work well as vases – I arranged these ones alongside a pretty vintage glass vase with a fluted edge found in a charity shop/thrift store (above). The flowers and foliage are from the garden, with the bright orange nasturtiums popping against the plywood walls. This detail (left) demonstrates how different woods work well against a plywood background.

natural timber cladding *Experiment with wooden wall treatments.*

Cladding interior walls with timber enables you to forgo such things as plasterboard/drywall, lining paper, wallpaper and paint. Plywood is an engineered wood product that has become a popular wall treatment in recent years, as it's relatively cheap and durable and has an interesting finish that gives interiors an on-trend feel. It's important to seek out FSC-certified plywood, which is made from sustainable sources and doesn't come from endangered rainforests. Eco plywood is also available, using glues with lower-VOC and formaldehyde emissions in the production process. From a styling point of view, plywood makes a great backdrop for a stylish seating area such as this one in Boskoop, Holland, where vintage rattan armchairs surround a folding table and stools made from reclaimed wood. Timber walls have a natural warming effect, and mixing different woods for floors, shelving and furniture will create a cosy, inviting interior.

DANISH PINE

Danish garden designer and TV presenter Dorthe Kvist and her husband recently built an extension/addition to their summerhouse north of Copenhagen to provide more living space. Their builder used sustainable pine sourced in Denmark to clad the internal walls and the result is this lovely room, a perfect spot to soak up the forest views beyond.

 MAKE natural firelighters

To make these firelighters (left), you will need soy wax flakes, small metal tart tins/pans and natural finds such as pine cones, dry leaves, twigs, lavender sprigs, dried berries, straw and wood shavings. Preheat your oven to 170°C/325°F. Fill each tin/pan with wax, then place them on a baking tray/sheet and pop it in the oven for 5 minutes or until the wax has melted. Remove the tray/sheet from the oven and push a variety of ingredients into each tin/pan of melted wax. Leave to set, then remove from the tins/pans and store in a dish near your stove or fire.

 MAKE a lavender soy candle

To make one candle, you will need soy wax flakes, an eco wick, an old saucepan, a long-handled spoon, a metal mini pudding mould and lavender flowers. Fill your mould with the wax flakes and empty into the saucepan, then repeat. Melt over a low heat, stirring occasionally. Once melted, set the wax aside to cool, then add the lavender (if you add the lavender when the wax is too hot, the scent will evaporate). Meanwhile, insert the wick into the bottom of the metal mould. Pour the lavender-infused wax into the container and leave overnight to set. The candle should pop out of the mould once set.

This muehlenbeckia plant in a stone planter sits in a salvaged metal dish on top of an old metal cabinet with glass doors (above). A grey loveseat is styled with linen cushions and a tactile sheepskin rug (right). The vintage metal factory lamp makes a great wall light, while plants add a botanical feel that softens the subtle grey tones.

salvaged style

Choose pieces with industrial vibes and a rich patina.

Using salvaged pieces is a great option when you want to freshen or restyle your interior without any negative impact on the environment. Finding redundant items that have been removed from homes, factories, offices or schools used to be about raiding skips/dumpsters and trawling junk shops, looking for treasure among other people's trash, but interesting and good-quality salvaged items are harder to find nowadays. There are, however, many companies that will do the rummaging and sourcing for you, so get to know your local salvage dealer or architectural reclamation yard. For Natural Living Style, items ideally need to be made from organic or sustainable materials such as wood, metal or stone. Susannah Le Mesurier, the owner of this gorgeous garden room, has furnished her space with items with a natural patina and worn details, sourced mostly from Baileys Home. Susannah's collection of houseplants introduces a living element that softens the space and – an added bonus – will also clean the air of pollutants.

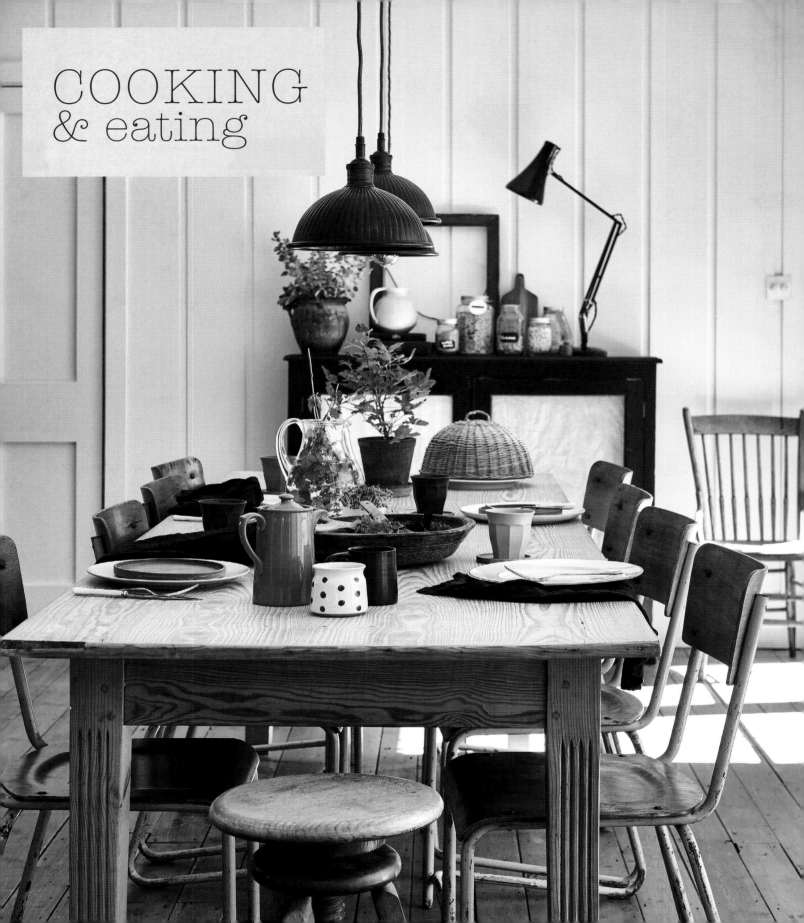

COOKING
& eating

Sending food to landfill is not only wasteful but also produces greenhouse gasses. Implement practical systems for kitchen waste: here, a metal bowl holds food scraps that are emptied daily onto a compost heap (above). Bottled water is a huge environmental burden, so give it up for tap and use garden herbs to infuse your drinks (right).

PLASTIC FREE
I love these stylish bamboo straws from the Zero Waste Club. Bamboo straws can be used again and again and will biodegrade when you have finished with them.

easy kitchen living

Get back to reality in the heart of the home.

Often said to be the heart of the home, the kitchen is at the centre of conscious decision-making when it comes to plastic-free choices and is perhaps the space where changes can be implemented fastest. There are tons of plastic-free alternatives for kitchen equipment, cookware, serveware and food storage, but this certainly doesn't mean you should throw out the plastic items that you already own. Instead, they should be used and reused until they are no longer fit for purpose. When you're in need of new things, aim to invest in items made from bamboo, wood, metal or other sustainable materials. When it comes to buying new tableware, choose pieces in colour tones that will work with the china, cutlery/flatware and furniture that you already have. Here, I have combined grey and white ceramic plates with a wooden dish perfect for serving salads, a rattan food cover that keeps bread fresh and a set of bamboo beakers by Nordal in earthy tones.

ZERO WASTE

Find out exactly what can be recycled in your area and what will be sent to landfill. Buying a new bin? Choose something made from metal if possible and aim to fill it as slowly as possible.

 MAKE glass food storage jars

Reuse glass food jars to store dry goods such as nuts, pulses, cereals and baking ingredients bought from bulk-buy plastic-free stores. First, sterilize the jars and lids – wash them in warm soapy water, then place them upside down on a clean baking tray/sheet and put into a preheated oven at 140˚C/275˚F for 10 minutes. If you are using jars with rubber seals, sterilize these separately by simmering in boiling water for 2–3 minutes. Let the jars cool before filling with food.

PLASTIC FREE

Open kitchen shelves mean things are permanently on show, so choose ceramic storage tubs with lids, recycle glass jars and look out for attractive vintage tins at second-hand shops/thrift stores.

LIGHT AND BRIGHT

This kitchen is full of natural details that create a homely vibe. Lighting is a central feature, with rattan lampshades suspended over the table and vintage Anglepoise lamps above the work surface to provide task lighting. A macramé curtain at the doorway keeps flies at bay during summer months.

 MAKE a hanging basket
for utensils & herbs

You will need two baskets, one larger
than the other, sturdy cord and scissors.
Calculate the desired drop of your basket,
then add extra to allow for the knots. Cut
three lengths of cord to the desired length,
then thread the first piece of cord through
the weave near the top rim of the biggest
basket and knot it firmly on the inside.
Repeat on the smaller basket, lining up the
knots. Repeat at regular intervals with the
other pieces of cord. Knot the three lengths
of cord together at the top and hang.

rustic country

A homespun look is achieved by mixing reclaimed woods with vintage furniture, a neutral palette and original details.

This rustic kitchen is at the heart of a charming country cottage originally built around 1600 for lime workers quarrying nearby. The current owner has sympathetically restored the kitchen in an authentic country style and it is now let out as a holiday home via Unique Home Stays. The built-in framework that houses the sink was constructed from reclaimed wood, while the marble worktop and curved splashback were lucky eBay finds. The wooden boards that clad the lower part of the wall were salvaged from an old village hall in Wales. Each board was studded with nails that were painstakingly removed before they were sanded and then waxed. Above these, simple shelves and a vintage plate rack have been hung. The neutral colour scheme on the walls and woodwork/trim extends to the china, enamelware and even the linen curtains that conceal the washing machine and dryer. The original floor tiles have been regrouted, bringing them back to their former glory. There's also space for a second-hand pine table that seats four comfortably and is surrounded by a mix of different chairs. The warm hues of mixed wood and organic textiles give the space a homely, cosy feel.

Open shelving is a good way to display tableware and vintage finds. Here, a metal rack fixed to the underside of a shelf is a good option for storing stemmed glasses. Appliances have been hidden behind a linen curtain that can be pulled aside when they are in use. Two fluted glass pendant shades suspended over the work space provide task lighting.

ZERO WASTE
Building a new kitchen?
How about using reclaimed
wood for cupboards and doors?
The rustic quality of reclaimed
wood is hard to replicate
with new wood.

HONEY HONEY
Is a country-style kitchen complete without a vase of garden flowers and a jar of local honey on the table (left and opposite)? These two items don't just look good – they also help to support bees, whose numbers are declining every year at an alarming rate due to drought, pesticides, pollution and habitat loss. We rely on bees to pollinate much of the food we eat, so it's important to help them wherever possible. Grow bee-friendly plants and flowers, install a bee hotel and buy local raw honey direct from beekeepers (below).

 MAKE a linen curtain

Linen's durability and strength make it a perfect choice for kitchen textiles. To create a simple curtain panel like this (above), you will need a piece of undyed raw linen, a sewing machine, cotton thread, scissors and clip-on metal curtain rings. Measure the height and width of the window to establish the size of your curtain. Add a 2.5cm/1-inch hem allowance to all sides. Cut the panel to the required size and hem all sides with a double-fold hem. Now press, attach the clip-on rings and hang.

 ## MAKE fabric food covers

Take a square of cotton fabric and place it
right side down on a table. Place a bowl on
the fabric, rim side down. Measure 5cm/
2 inches from the rim then mark a circle
around the bowl with a pencil. Cut out the
fabric circle. Place it wrong side up in your
sewing machine, with the raw edge under the
presser foot. Align a strip of elastic with the
raw edge and sew a few zigzag stitches to
secure it. Pull the elastic taut and continue
to zigzag stitch it to the edge, adjusting as you
go, until you have sewn all the way around.

Did you know that you can make delicious teas from garden plants? They are healthy and tasty. Since my trip to Boskoop, Holland, I've been making an infused tea with lemon mint, lemon verbena and lavender inspired by the botanical teas Debora Treep served us while we were there. Make your own flavours using pesticide-free home-grown herbs and edible flowers.

easy dining spaces

Create relaxed natural areas to eat in.

For me, there is nothing like gathering my nearest and dearest around our dining table and enjoying food and conversation. I love styling the table too, and flowers and foliage are my chosen ingredients when it comes to creating a centrepiece. I'm a fan of using mismatched chairs around a table – this works particularly well with second-hand chairs. The stunning space shown opposite is used purely for entertaining and there's even a couple of beds on the mezzanine floor for guests to retreat to after the party. It's owned by Debora Treep, a florist, garden designer and professor in nature management, and her husband Jan van Pelt, and was built using recycled materials as an extension/addition to the side of an old greenhouse in Boskoop, Holland, a town famous for its plant nurseries. This dining table sits in front of double doors looking out over a canal. It's the perfect spot for tea and homemade cakes on vintage plates! If you need a new dining table, pick one made with FSC-certified wood, which guarantees that it was grown and harvested responsibly.

STYLE TIP
Display treasured flea-market china and tableware on dressers or in display cabinets. Paint the interior white and the pieces will stand out. When painting furniture, always use eco-friendly low-VOC paints.

SLEEPING
& washing

soft pastel linens

Create a stylish, soft and serene sleeping space.

Our bedrooms and bathrooms are private spaces where we rest, recuperate and cleanse. Be mindful of colour choices in these areas, as they will have an impact on the mood of the space. Soft pastels are a lovely choice because they evoke a calm, restful feel – think earthy pink combined with rust, olive green and grey. If you opt for ethically produced clothes, why not investigate environmentally friendly bedding too? Cotton production takes a heavy toll on the environment, requiring huge amounts of water, pesticides and insecticides, and has been linked with child labour. Linen is made from the fibres of the flax plant, and although its production is less polluting than that of cotton, it is often heavily bleached, so try to track down natural linen. Organic cotton and linen bedding is perfect for anyone with skin allergies, as it is not treated with chemicals to make it 'easy iron' or quick drying. Many big brands sell organic cotton bedding, while smaller companies offer organic cotton bedding plus wool pillows and duvets. Look for the GOTS (Global Organic Textile Standard) certification.

Dark elements will ground pastel schemes and introduce a more sophisticated note. Consider a black linen headboard or a wooden lamp base stained black. This bed is dressed with a grey linen throw that's actually a tablecloth from H&M (above). The joy of linen bedding is that it looks even better when it's softly wrinkled (opposite).

PLASTIC FREE
*Swap plastic bottles of liquid
soap for bars handmade with
essential oils. Reuse glass jars
for storing beauty accessories
such as these biodegradable
bamboo cotton buds
by Hydrophil.*

ECO-FRIENDLY ACCESSORIES

*Rattan rugs are the perfect natural addition to
the bathroom, softening a tiled floor (opposite).
Linen bath towels absorb moisture quickly and feel
pleasant against the skin. Storage baskets keep
things neat on open shelves, while plants enhance
the space (left). A vintage bamboo magazine rack
works well as a side table and would be a good
place to store spare towels. Look out for plastic-
free beauty products, such as bamboo cotton buds
(above), charcoal dental floss by Georganics and
reusable facecloths rather than disposable wipes.*

Is a favourite rug looking a little worn or threadbare? Adopt the make-do-and-mend approach and patch it (above). Choose a piece of fabric in a similar shade to the rug, and cut out a patch that's large enough to cover any holes. A wall-mounted hook board makes a good place to select outfits for the week (left).

coastal colours

Think crashing waves, grey rocks and frothy surf.

A colour scheme inspired by nature always creates a tranquil vibe. If you warm to muted hues, opt for a scheme that draws on moody blue seas, soft grey skies and beach pebbles. The bedroom and bathroom shown on these pages are particularly on-trend in their use of warm greys combined with simple, natural elements, such as wooden stools put into service as bedside tables/nightstands and found elements used as decoration. The walls are a calm off-white – the perfect backdrop for the subdued tones of the bedlinen, the iron tub and the wooden detailing. No headboard is required on the bed, as a heap of large cushions in linen covers provides a touch of luxurious comfort. Behind the tub, a battered but beautiful console table is home to an old French mirror and a display of dried seaweeds. Want to recreate this look? Choose a palette of soft, dull blues grounded with grey and rustic woods, and keep it simple – interesting textures adds all the necessary visual interest here. Look for items with an aged patina – worn wood or driftwood will both work well.

ZERO WASTE

Showering uses less water than taking a bath, but every now and then a bath is a relaxing treat. Use your bath water to water houseplants – simply scoop it out with a watering can.

ALL WASHED OUT

Paint-effect walls were popular in the 1990s and are making a comeback. Achieve a similar result to the one shown on this page by using a rag to apply a watery wash of organic paint to a wall. Unlike some other fabrics, linens improve with age. For an easy, breezy coastal home effect, it doesn't matter if sheets and duvet covers fade or are slightly mismatched (opposite).

STYLE TIP

Seagrass matting is a
sustainable way to add comfort
and warmth in the bedroom.
Seagrass is a natural, renewable
resource. It is sustainable, as it
grows quickly and abundantly.
It is also biodegradable
and carbon neutral.

SPACE SAVING

This room is a true multi-purpose space, as the iron bed, when not in use, can be hauled up and suspended from the ceiling using a pulley system (opposite). The bedding – a mix of vintage bedspreads, organic cotton sheets and woven blankets with a decorative pom pom trim – is stored in the cupboard.

Some of my favourite natural skincare products are a sandalwood, immortelle and Roman chamomile moisturiser by Shizen Remedies and the rosehip and clay facial mask from Formulary 55. If you're interested in learning about natural remedies for skincare, you might like to attend a workshop with an aromatherapy specialist or organization such as Neal's Yard that offers courses where you can make your own skincare.

natural bathing

Combine stone with reclaimed wood and new eco products.

The bathroom can be more than a functional area– it can also be a space to relax and unwind. Natural materials give bathrooms a warm, organic feel. This bathtub is boxed in with reclaimed wooden panel cladding, and although it has been sanded so that it is smooth to the touch, it still has an intriguing patina. The bathroom is another area where going plastic free can have serious impact on the amount of waste your household generates. From toothpaste tubes to shampoo bottles, our bathrooms are heaving with plastic, and the statistic that only 9% of the plastic ever made has been recycled is shocking. Kickstart your own personal anti-plastic regime by choosing organic natural beauty products sold in reusable and recyclable glass bottles and jars rather than plastic ones that are likely to land up in landfill. To minimize waste even more, experiment with making your own beauty and cleaning products with essential oils for natural fragrance and healing qualities. Organic pine oil will give bathrooms a natural botanical scent when used in homemade cleaning sprays.

 MAKE *natural toothpaste*

There's no need to buy toothpaste in tubes when you can so easily make your own (left). In a glass jar that has a tight-fitting lid, mix 2 tablespoons of organic coconut oil, 1 tablespoon of baking soda and 6 drops of peppermint oil, 6 drops of lemon oil and 6 drops of tea tree oil. Mix well. Another benefit of making your own toothpaste is that you can put it in a glass jar container that can be reused.

WORK
SPACES
& studios

If you commute or head out for meetings, invest in a cup for coffee on the run. I work from home or on location, but often travel into London for meetings and press reviews. Disposable coffee cups are currently not recyclable, which causes huge amounts of waste. Take your own cup and most places will also offer you a discount on your coffee. I love these bamboo takeaway cups by Ecoffee (above).

salvage chic

Furnish your work space with salvaged items for a unique effect.

This home office has a relaxed industrial vibe that's perfectly suited to the Natural Living Style home. To achieve a similar effect, mix aged and rustic wood with old metal elements for an easy-going look that takes inspiration from architectural salvage and reclamation. The result has a timeless appeal – everything is slightly worn, and each piece has been collected over time. Look out for original items salvaged from defunct shops, factories, offices or schools. Smaller pieces like metal deed boxes with hinged lids and wooden cubbyholes make for interesting and versatile storage. The desk is easy to erect and move, as it's simply two thick planks of salvaged wood resting on two rustic wood trestles – a vintage wallpaper-pasting table would be a good alternative. The vintage wood and leather office chair adds comfort and style, and the collection of decorative type personalizes the space. Wire baskets are used as in- and out-trays and a recycling bin.

STYLE TIP
I love Pinterest, but a good
old-fashioned pinboard looks
great on the wall – rip out
anything that inspires you and
pin it up before sending your
magazines and newspapers
to the recycling bin.

LIGHT AND AIRY

This overhead light has a long arm that can be manoeuvred across the table to wherever task lighting is necessary. The skylights allow natural light to flood into the room and can be opened to fill the space with fresh air too.

An upstairs landing with a large window is a pleasant spot for a work space – a simple table plus a couple of chairs are all that is needed (left). I always add natural greenery for a botanical feel, while plants will purify the air; some good options include spider plants, trailing ivy and philodendrons. Add decorative elements, like this rusted metal ampersand from RE-Found Objects that hangs from a framed picture found in a charity shop/thrift store (above).

nooks & corners

Forge an area to work in even if space is tight.

When it comes to working from home, any nook and corner can be turned into a functional work space as long as there's room for a desk and chair. The most sustainable type of lighting is natural light, so position your desk under or next to a window. Access to fresh air (and perhaps a leafy view) will also be beneficial. Keep things simple – install any necessary tech, but draw the line at plastic folders and cheap ballpoints. I have invested in pens made from recycled plastic, along with folders and notebooks made of recycled paper. Baskets or boxes holding files or stationery or for recycling can be stowed away under the desk. Before heading out to buy new furniture, look for second-hand office furniture that you can upcycle if necessary. I found an old wooden filing cabinet several years ago and it has moved around with me, taking up residence in all my home offices. If you have no access to natural light or if you are tucked away in a dark corner, you will require effective task lighting – choose a desk lamp that works with energy-efficient LED bulbs.

This alcove to one side of the chimneybreast in an old Dutch farmhouse has the original wooden structure of the house on show, while the white-painted walls and ceiling keep the space fresh and bright (left). Light floods in from the glazed doors at one side and a small internal window. The desk is an antique table in dark stained wood, and the bright green chair is a classic Eames design from the 1950s – a piece to be treasured.

 ## MAKE wax lunch bags

To make this lunch bag, you will need cotton fabric and basic sewing supplies. Cut two rectangles of fabric measuring 25 x 15cm/10 x 6 inches. Cut 5cm/2½-inch squares from the two corners of the short end of each rectangle. With right sides facing, stitch the two pieces together at the sides and bottom (leave the cut-out squares). Now bring the square corners together and pin them before sewing in place, then turn the bag right side out. To wax the bag, melt beeswax and use a clean brush to apply warm wax to all surfaces inside and out of the bag. Hang to dry.

Shopping
~ Milk
~ Eggs
~ Jam
~ Post Office
~ Stamps
~ envelopes

MAKE newspaper decorations

Make natural tree decorations from old papers. You will need cardboard (use an old box), newspaper cut into small squares, scissors, PVA glue, a glue brush and a needle and thread. Cut a heart, star or any shape you like from the cardboard. Push the needle and thread through the top of the shape to create a hanging loop. Take small squares of newspaper and glue them all over the card shape until it's covered (you may need several layers). Hang to dry, then arrange decoratively on a branch.

STYLE TIP
If your work space is housed in an open-plan interior or is at one end of a room so that you can't close the door on it at the end of the working day, then hang a linen curtain to close off the space during downtime.

A deep windowsill becomes a handy place to store decorating samples, fabrics and surface materials, and the view onto the courtyard is a welcome one even on a rainy day (left). Utilize any available areas – windowsills, tops of cabinets and shelves – for display or storage space. A wooden pencil is the go-to tool for the daily crossword (above).

creative spaces

An interior designer's tranquil home office space.

If you work from home, it's important to consider the following factors when you create your ideal work space: natural light, fresh air, a comfy chair and recycling systems for paper and other waste. This fabulous high-ceilinged space in London belongs to interior designer Beth Dadswell of Imperfect Interiors and is pretty much the dream home office-cum-studio. It boasts a huge window overlooking a compact courtyard and a skylight above that floods the room with natural light – entirely sustainable and essential when making design decisions on paint samples and fabric swatches. Built-in storage runs all the way around the walls, creating a handy work surface. A collection of moodboards relating to work in progress are propped up against the far wall. The cushioned retro-style brown velvet office chair was a second-hand buy, while various baskets make ideal storage for bits and pieces, including paper recycling. The walls are eco-friendly lime plaster, with the beamed ceiling adding visual interest.

UTILITY ROOMS &
practical spaces

Garden Trading (gardentrading.co.uk) is my first choice for well-designed, practical staples for the laundry area and utility room. They offer wooden brushes and baskets for stylish storage, and their ceiling dryer or beechwood folding clothes horse is ideal for drying clothes inside (above left and right). Install hooks on a wall or door for storing items when not in use (opposite).

washday simplicity

Go back to basics on laundry day.

Want a stylish area in which to do your laundry? Even the smallest space can be given an eco-friendly makeover. For storage, choose natural fibre baskets over plastic tubs, while metal dustpans and wooden-handled brushes with natural bristles last longer than their plastic counterparts. Tumble dryers have a huge carbon footprint, so air-dry outside if you possibly can – it's better for your clothes and the planet. Even a tiny laundry area will allow you to air-dry inside when outside drying is not an option. Folding wooden dryers are sturdier than plastic versions and look nicer too. Hanging ceiling dryers work brilliantly when space is tight; this one (above left) was custom-made to hold large sheets and has been passed down through the family. Washing machines are not the most eco-friendly of appliances, so try to wash your clothes on a cool cycle, fully load your machine and opt for green detergent sold in recyclable or refillable containers.

MAKE knitted dishcloths

Nanna Peggy, my husband's nanna, was the knitted dishcloth queen – she used to make loads, which she sold to raise money for her local community. Made from 100% cotton yarn, knitted dishcloths are eco-friendly, as they can be washed and reused again and again, providing the perfect alternative to synthetic sponges and cloths. To make your own, you will need knitting needles, some cotton yarn/craft cotton and basic knitting skills. Start by casting 26 stitches onto your needle, knit 26 rows using garter stitch to form a square, then cast off.

MAKE a natural cleaning spray

I buy most of my cleaning and beauty products from shizenremedies.com, a small, local-to-me company that makes natural products and offers a reusable container service. Seek out businesses close to you that offer a similar service or make your own all-purpose non-toxic cleaning spray. Mix 2 cups of filtered water, 1 cup of organic distilled white vinegar and 6 drops each of lavender oil, lemon oil and peppermint oil all together in a spray bottle and label clearly.

EVERYTHING IN ITS PLACE
Keep your utility space organized with a practical trolley. This movable example – the birch Förhöja from IKEA – is a good option, with handy shelves for items you don't want on show and drawers for smaller bits and pieces. The galvanized metal bins alongside are smart options for a stylish recycling system.

MAKE a drawstring peg bag

Cut a piece of fabric measuring approximately 25 x 34cm/10 x 13½ inches. Hem both the shorter sides. Fold over 2cm/½ inch of one longer end and hem in place. Now fold down this hemmed edge by another 5cm/2 inches and pin in place. Sew along the folded edge to create a channel for the drawstring. Fold the piece of fabric in two with right sides facing. Sew neatly around the sides and bottom, leaving a gap at the top where your channel is. Turn right side out, then thread a piece of cord through the channel and knot the ends to stop it slipping out. Fill with pegs.

TRADITIONAL SOLUTIONS

I have an array of baskets from basketbasket.co.uk that I use for a variety of different tasks – they work as laundry baskets as well as shopping bags and stylish storage (above). If you need to prop up your washing line, head to the woods in search of a long stick with a forked top – it will do the job nicely (opposite). Knitted coat hangers will protect delicate clothing and I love the natural, earthy colours of these ones (right). For similar, try Etsy.com

green housekeeping

Choose eco-friendly cleaning products for your home.

If you walk along the household-cleaning aisle of your local supermarket, you will see a vast array of plastic bottles containing commercial cleaning products that are among the most toxic products found in the home. You'll also see plastic cloths (wrapped in yet more plastic) and plastic dustpans and brushes and dishwashing bowls. My hope is that in the future big brands and supermarkets will embrace eco-friendly formulations and try to use less plastic, or at least offer plastic-free alternatives – wooden-handled scrubbing brushes with natural bristles, metal buckets instead of plastic ones and natural cleaning sprays in refillable glass bottles. Although such items are not available in all supermarkets, things are changing – there are plenty of green products nowadays and wooden brushes are sold by independent companies and online. Some of these items will be more expensive than their plastic counterparts, but will last a long time and are more planet friendly. New-to-market items include coconut scrubbers, bamboo dish drainers and cleaning pads made from loofah plants.

The wood-clad walls of this utility room have been adorned with oak peg rails with leather hooks designed by Danish company by Wirth (above). The pegs are a great place to hang linen and canvas shopping bags along with a Feuer lantern and linen tea towel. A wooden cupboard keeps a selection of naturally simple utility items stored away (opposite).

ZERO WASTE
Fill (fillrefill.co) is a company on a mission to produce refillable eco-friendly laundry and cleaning products that look good, work brilliantly and reduce packaging.

WASH AND BRUSH-UP

When they need replacing, swap plastic brushes for versions made from wood and natural fibres (left and above left). Choose washable, reusable bamboo wipes over plastic-wrapped kitchen roll/ paper towels and try out EcoCoconut scourers made from coconut coir, which is a natural fibre extracted from between the internal shell and the outer coat of the coconut. As well as being totally natural, the scourers are antibacterial, free from toxic chemicals, recyclable and biodegradable. Fill's bergamot floor cleaner smells divine (above).

NATURAL
outdoor spaces

OUTDOOR
living

Locally sourced Welsh stone slabs have been used to fashion this terrace in the riverside garden owned by Susannah Le Mesurier, situated in a pretty Welsh village by the River Wye (opposite). In Denmark, Dorthe Kvist's wooden deck mirrors the overhanging roof above, which offers shade in the summer and shelter from downpours (left). A well-stocked wood store in this Dutch garden makes a lovely backdrop for a seating area (above).

terraces & verandahs

Carve out a sustainable space to dine and relax.

Taking an eco-friendly approach to decorating your interior can be continued outdoors. Outside areas that can be used for eating, entertaining and relaxing are a brilliant way to extend your living space. Even the smallest area has potential, as long as you can squeeze in a folding chair and a table. Sourcing sustainable materials to build verandahs, pergolas, patios and terraces can be time-consuming and more expensive than heading for a DIY store. Explore recycled materials, or reuse materials that you already have to hand. Perhaps a neglected terrace could be jet-washed and repointed, with any broken slabs replaced, or salvaged wood or metal sheeting refashioned into a lean-to or roof for a garden structure. Old scaffolding boards make excellent rustic-style decking. If you need to source new wood, stone or metal, buy from companies with excellent ethical credentials and make sure that the wood comes from legal and sustainable sources. The same goes for garden furniture – buying unprotected timber may destroy primary forest.

PLASTIC FREE
Furnish your terrace or
verandah with pieces made from
FSC-certified wood or second-
hand bamboo or rattan seating.
Decorate with natural
woven mats and paper
lanterns.

NORDIC INSPIRATION

For centuries, buildings throughout the Nordic region have been
painted to protect them from the harsh winter weather. The
popular richly coloured paint known as Falu red was historically
made from pigments that were a by-product of the mining
industry at Falun in Dalarna, Sweden. In Denmark, Anna and
Lars of The Norrmans B&B inherited a barn painted in Falu red.
It has a covered verandah and is now used for outdoor parties
and celebrations (above and left). The Lindeborgs' 100-year-old
Eco Barn has acquired a new verandah, but traditional red paint
has been applied, marrying the old and new together (opposite).

garden hideaways & conservatories

Create nooks and crannies for inspiration and relaxation.

What is it about spaces in nature where you can hide out, relax or socialize? When I'm visiting gardens, plant nurseries or hotels with outdoor areas, I'm always most inspired by the garden rooms, greenhouses and potting sheds. It's reassuring to see these inviting spaces filled with decorative bits and pieces: plants, flowers in vases and windowsills that are home to lanterns, baskets or plant pots. A greenhouse or conservatory, if roomy enough, can act as a seating area and a place to grow plants at the same time. At the Worton Organic Garden in Oxfordshire, UK, a huge fig tree grows happily in the conservatory that houses their on-site café, while a shepherd's hut offers a cute hideaway. The Norrmans B&B in Denmark has a cabin made from reclaimed wood and windows, which is used as a space to chill out in, while in Boskoop, Holland, an old greenhouse has been converted into a party venue. Each of these spaces is furnished sympathetically with eco-friendly items such as rattan chairs, bamboo tables and daybeds covered in natural textiles.

The Worton Organic Garden in Oxfordshire, UK, is a heavenly place to visit and gather inspiration (opposite and above). Their styling is always on point, with beautiful displays of seasonal flowers and foliage, they have a few different areas to sit and relax, and the menu in their café is inspired by what they organically grow on the land.

STYLE TIP
Need to create shade in your greenhouse or conservatory? Make blinds by draping willow or rattan screening across bamboo struts. Use jute string to attach the bamboo and screening to the frame of your structure.

UNDER GLASS
At The Norrmans B&B in Denmark, this charming cabin is filled with retro rattan furniture. The door and windows are salvaged pieces (this page). An old greenhouse in Holland is now a venue for classes on gardening and parties at the weekends (opposite).

Under a black-painted pergola at the Worton Organic Garden, a round metal table is teamed with wooden and metal folding chairs (opposite). When not in use for dining, the table is a display area, with an antique stone head as a centrepiece and vases of freshly cut flowers and upturned terracotta plant pots surrounding it.

outdoor seating

Embrace natural weathering effects on garden furniture.

When it comes to garden furniture, I'm happy to let my vintage metal table and chairs develop a little rust over time – it only adds to their charm. Wood, wicker and rattan seating, however, will not withstand all weathers, so store it in a shed or garage during the winter months. Just like the kitchen and dining-room tables, the garden table also deserves a decorative centrepiece. Rattan or wicker trays look lovely with an array of different pots and plants arranged on them – ornate stone urns with rustic handmade planters, for example. In the summer months, homeware stores and supermarkets are awash with garden accessories, including plastic tableware and utensils, but I always use our regular glassware and tableware in the garden. If you are worried about pieces getting broken, look for tableware made from bamboo, which is a renewable resource. Danish company Nordal has produced a range in an appealing mix of earthy greys and taupes.

 MAKE tree stump seats & table

Get in touch with a local tree surgeon and ask if they are able to supply you with tree stumps. You will need two sturdy tree stumps of roughly the same height (35–40cm/14–16 inches approximately) for the seats, and a third stump that's slightly taller for the base of the table. You will also need a square piece of chunky oak measuring roughly 60 x 60cm/ 2 x 2 feet (ideally sourced from a wood yard or salvage yard) for the tabletop. Position the stumps in your desired spot, then use four L-shaped stainless-steel brackets to attach the oak table top on top of the taller stump.

 MAKE an outdoor cork sofa

Cork is a sustainable natural product that is both renewable and recyclable. This sofa (above) was made using semi-rigid cork insulation blocks and sheets. First construct four columns from cork blocks, then place a sheet of cork over them to form a seat. Another large sheet was used to make the back, which is propped against a wall. This sofa is positioned under a covered verandah, so is sheltered from the weather and has been dressed with a Moroccan rug and cushion.

NATURAL gardens

Work areas are one of my favourite parts of the garden – I love a utilitarian shed or covered work bench. These hard-working spaces are key to keeping the garden ticking over and often house the garden waste recycling bins and the all-important compost heap. In a tucked-away corner of your garden, add green systems to help you garden more organically (opposite).

green gardening

Find natural ways to garden while nuturing plants and wildlife.

If I am ever asked to go to my 'happy place' in my mind, it's always a beautiful garden brimming with flowers, with bumble bees buzzing and butterflies landing on blowsy blooms. I have been lucky enough to visit lots of inspiring gardens with these qualities, and I'm trying to make our own garden match the one in my botanical daydream. Although gardening, by definition, is cultivating nature, there are plenty of ways to do this in an eco-friendly fashion. As we now know, plastic is not so fantastic, so it's no longer acceptable to buy plants in plastic pots, then discard them. Some nurseries will take back empty pots, but it's more sustainable to grow plants from seed, take cuttings or buy plants sold in biodegradable pots. It's important to grow plants that are suited to the conditions in your garden, as they will require less watering, fertilizer and pesticide. Water is not an infinite resource and we should all do our best to conserve it, so if you're a keen gardener, consider fitting a water butt to a downpipe to collect rainwater – perfect for watering the garden.

First and foremost, green gardening means using no chemicals. To combat pests like slugs and snails, try natural wool slug pellets or fix copper tape around the rim of pots or raised beds. It's a good idea to leave wild areas in the garden for wildlife, and you can benefit too by creating a meadow area dotted with wild flowers like buttercups, daisies and poppies. It will save you from having to mow the lawn! Finally, no organic garden is complete without a composting system (below).

 MAKE a cold frame from a salvaged window

You will need an old window in a frame from a skip/ dumpster or your local salvage yard. Measure the window, as this will dictate the size of your raised bed. Build your cold frame to these measurements using FSC-certified wood. Note that you will need to create angled sides so that the frame is slanted. Paint the frame with Eco Wood Treatment. Then attach your window using two strong hinges at the top (above). It's a good idea to affix a sturdy prop to hold the window up when required.

ZERO WASTE

Save rainwater by installing a water butt or tank. They are easy to attach to any building – think house, shed or garage – that already has guttering and a downpipe.

MAKE recycled card seed pots

Cardboard egg cartons and toilet paper rolls are ideal for growing from seed (below). Fill the individual cups in the base of an egg carton with seed compost and stand the cardboard rolls in the lid of the carton before filling each one with compost. Sow seeds into each compartment as per the packet instructions. Label, water well and leave to germinate, maintaining a temperature of around 18˚C/64˚F. Once the seedlings are ready to plant, the rolls can be planted directly into the soil/dirt, as they will biodegrade. The carton base will break into sections that can also be planted directly into the ground.

With their tall stalks and long flowering season, hollyhocks are an old-fashioned cottage-garden favourite. Their open flowers are very bee friendly, and left to their own devices the plants will naturally self-seed, popping up in new spots each year. I particularly like the dramatic black-coloured varieties such as Black Knight (above).

attracting wildlife

Green gardens are full of all forms of life.

Biodiversity may sound complicated, but put simply it means that all life forms on our planet interact with each other and the physical environment around us. For example, we need plants to produce oxygen, while it is estimated that bees pollinate a third of the global food supply. So growing a large number of different plant species and encouraging wildlife into your garden is very desirable. To attract birds that help with pest control, erect nest boxes and put out bird food, especially during the winter months. The single fastest way to add wildlife to a garden is to install a pond, however tiny – a trough, large pot or an old tub in an out-of-the-way spot will do. Entice bees by choosing plants with open, showy blooms that flower year-round, and build a bee hotel – the perfect home for solitary bees. Leave some parts of the garden untidy – nature likes it messy, so heap leaves in undisturbed corners and pile up logs and branches. You'll encourage thousands of insects, while foraging birds and small mammals will also find such spots irresistible.

HAPPY INSECTS
This cute little timber and glass greenhouse overlooks a garden in Holland that is rich in wildlife and where insects are enjoying a rich mix of perennial and annual blooms (left). This old lean-to made from salvaged corrugated metal sheets can be found in the garden of Apifera holiday cottage (via Unique Home Stays). It's surrounded by a wildlife-rich habitat of plants and trees (opposite left).

HEMP GARDEN TOTE
Eco-friendly hemp fabric is perfect for a garden tote like this (right). Cut five pieces of hemp fabric, one 35 x 50 cm/ 14 x 20 inches for the base, two 25 x 35 cm/10 x 14 inches for the ends, and two 25 x 50 cm/10 x 20 inches for the sides. You will also need two 60cm/2-foot lengths of webbing for the handles. Hem each piece of hemp then sew the two end pieces to the base with right sides facing. Repeat to attach the sides, then sew the corners together inside to make a rectangular tote. Stitch the webbing inside each side. Find something similar at Ragged Home via Etsy.

Whatever you grow, you're likely to have a glut of one particular item at some time, so seek out preserving recipes and make sure nothing goes to waste. Most fruits and vegetables can be made into delicious soups, chutneys and sauces that can be stored in sterilized and sealed glass jars. I like the idea of recycling old shoe laces for tying plants to support canes (above).

a productive plot

Grow your own chemical-free, packaging-free crops.

Growing your own food will give you fresh vegetables and fruits that haven't been sprayed with chemicals or wrapped in plastic. It's true that having a productive plot is something of an investment in terms of time and patience – there will be lots of digging over, replanting, watering and nurturing required – but boy, is it worth it. Inspired by French potager gardens, it's fashionable now to grow edible plants in flowerbeds alongside herbs and cut-and-come-again flowers, and this is a good option if space is limited. If you want to make your veggie patch appealing to spend time in, add an old table that can be used as a potting bench, and a bench or couple of seats so that you have somewhere to sit and admire the fruits of your labours. Look out for old gardening tools at car boot/yard sales – something with wooden handles will be much nicer to use than a modern version made of garish plastic. If this all sounds like too much hard work, or you don't have any space to grow things, buy home-grown produce from a local farmers' market or local grower instead.

PLASTIC FREE
Investigate plastic-free options for the vegetable patch. Glass cloches look nicer than plastic domes for protecting seedlings. Don't buy soil/dirt in plastic bags – get it delivered by the truck load.

grown not flown

Support local flower farms and experiment with growing your own blooms.

I am always amazed by the huge array of beautiful blooms that can be grown on quite a small scale. I have been encouraged to grow my own flowers by Worton Organic Garden, Green & Gorgeous and many other flower growers I have met, and in recent years I have had great success cultivating chocolate cosmos, sweet peas, *Ammi majus*, foxgloves, lupins, dahlias and edible flowers in my garden.

Apparently, 90% of flowers sold in the UK are imported and have a large carbon footprint. Imports tend to be mass cultivated in huge glasshouses, many in developing countries, and are sprayed with chemical preservatives so they survive their journey to their point of sale. It's well worth buying locally grown flowers wherever possible. Like home-grown or locally grown veg that are fresher and taste better, locally grown flowers usually have a better fragrance and last longer than their well-travelled counterparts. If you choose scented flowers, they will add a delicate floral note to your space too.

Wondering how to style and arrange a bunch of flowers? Garden blooms often look better when loosely arranged in a simple glass or ceramic vessel, which allows their beauty to shine through.

GLEANING FLORAL INSPIRATION

Not comfortable with arranging blooms yourself? Find a local florist who can put together something special for an occasion or gift. This arrangement (left) was created by Joolz Abbs-Woodd (@posyflowersandgifts) for the LA-EVA studio in Oxfordshire, while these freshly picked flowers are on display at the Worton Organic Garden (above and opposite). There is an array of talented florists out there who can source and style flowers for you, many of them to be found via Instagram. A few of my favourites are @wintersworkshop, @juneinmarch, @gandgorgeousflowers and @flowersfromthefarm.

SEASONAL DECORATION
Draw from nature to create an array of natural decorations for your home, including wreaths, scented posies and garlands (opposite). Use seasonal flowers and foliage bought or gathered from a sustainable source. Wreaths made from flowers that look good when dried, like these hydrangeas, are a great option, as they last a lot longer (left).

 MAKE a natural wreath

To make this wreath (above) you will need natural materials sourced from your own garden or sustainably foraged and a wicker or willow wreath base from a floral supplies shop. You can use fresh or dried natural material, flowers, foliage and berries – for this wreath, I used dried hydrangea heads, lavender and seedheads from my garden. Take the wreath base and insert and thread the dried flowers and foliage into gaps in the base until you are happy with the results.

sources

SELINA LAKE
Stylist and author
+44 (0)7971447785
www.selinalake.co.uk
Social media @selinalake

&KEEP
www.andkeep.com
A great resource for plastic-free living and parenting. Eco-friendly, reusable and sustainable products for home and body include EcoCoconut biodegradable scrubbers, Hydrophil bamboo cotton buds and Georganics charcoal dental floss and toothpaste.

&HOBBS
www.andhobbs.com
A lovely independent homeware store in the stunning village of Shere in the Surrey hills, UK. Libby Hobbs, the owner of the venture, has a great eye for pieces made from sustainable materials and celebrates local makers and designers.

&TRADITION
www.andtradition.com
Danish design store featuring elegantly functional lighting, furniture and accessories.

ALSO HOME
www.alsohome.com
Lovely home decor, furnishings and home accessories made from natural materials. Their range includes bed linen, seagrass placemats and ceramics.

AURO
www.auro-uk.com
High quality, breathable paints, wood stains, floor oils, furniture waxes and decorative finishes that are sustainably produced and petrochemical free.

BASKET BASKET
www.basketbasket.co.uk
French baskets, straw shopping baskets and African market baskets; eco-friendly, handmade and fair trade.

THE BASKET ROOM
www.thebasketroom.com
Colourful handwoven sisal baskets made by small craft collectives in Africa. Stylish, handmade and fair trade.

BAUWERK
www.bauwerk.com
Modern lime paint company offering a range of stylish and environmentally friendly paints entirely made from natural products.

BYWIRTH
www.bywirth.dk
Danish-designed products made from FSC-certified wood and leather.

ECOFFEE
www.ecoffeecup.eco
Reusable Coffee Cups made with natural bamboo fibre.

ETSY
www.etsy.com
Handmade and vintage goods. Shop hemp trug bags and hessian storage bags by Ragged Home, botanical screenprints by Aimee Mac Illustration and raw linen tablecloths, napkins, shopper bags and hemp backpacks by ScandaloAlSole.

FABCO SANCTUARY
www.fabcosanctuary.com
Bespoke steel-framed windows and doors with a certified B-thermal rating as standard.

FALCON ENAMELWARE
www.falconenamel.com
Traditional enamelware that will last a lifetime.

FARROW & BALL
www.farrow-ball.com
Water-based, low-VOC paints in subtle shades.

FILL
www.fillrefill.co
Eco household cleaning and laundry products in refillable glass bottles.

FORMULARY 55
www.formulary55.com
Cruelty free vegan products for body and home.

GARDEN TRADING
www.gardentrading.co.uk
Stylish items for your home and garden.

IKEA
www.ikea.com
Selection of cork, seagrass and sisal products and natural wood furniture. IKEA is striving for sustainability in everything they do and the company is working towards sourcing only renewable, recyclable or recycled materials.

JAMES HARE
www.james-hare.com
Designer fabrics including silks and linens.

KONSTHANTVERK
www.konsthantverk.com
Elegant Swedish lighting that's designed and manufactured to last for many generations.

LA-EVA
www.la-eva.com
Organic, cruelty free skincare products and scents packaged in glass and made in England.

LOUISA MAYBURY
4 Market Street
Woodstock
Oxfordshire OX20 1SX
+44 (0)1993 818814
www.louisamaybury.co.uk
Antique Moroccan and Turkish rugs, textiles, Indian kilims and cactus silk cushions.

MADAM STOLTZ
www.madamstoltz.dk
Danish home accessories in natural materials such as bamboo, organic cotton and palm leaf.

MARTHA'S ATTIC
17 Oxford Street
Woodstock
Oxfordshire OX20 1TH
+44 (0)1993 813301
www.marthasattic.co.uk
Decorative antiques and reclaimed window mirrors.

MELO STUDIO
www.melostudio.se
Elegant handcrafted furniture made in Sweden from ash wood.

NATURAL BEDROOM
www.naturalbedroom.co.uk
Organic cotton bedding, wool-filled duvets and pillows.

NATURAL MAT
www.naturalmat.co.uk
Organic natural fibre or pocket sprung mattresses made by hand in the UK plus luxury organic cotton bedding and nursery items.

NEAL'S YARD REMEDIES
www.nealsyardremedies.com
Pioneers in natural and organic skincare with an ethical and sustainable ethos. Made in England and packaged in glass. Courses available in natural health, beauty and wellbeing.

NORDAL
www.nordal.eu
Family-run furniture and home accessories company. Look out for their range of bamboo kitchenware.

PACKAGE-FREE SHOP
www.packagefreeshop.com
US-based zero-waste package-free shop offering everything that's needed for a low-waste lifestyle.

RE-FOUND OBJECTS
www.re-foundobjects.com
Recycled, rescued and restored furniture and objects for the home.

SHEPHERD'S DREAM
wwwshepherdsdream.com
GOTS-certified organic cotton bedding plus wool mattresses, toppers, comforters and blankets.

SHIZEN REMEDIES
www.shizenremedies.com
Beautiful natural products for mind, body and home. They are passionate about reusing and recycling (packaging many of their products in glass) and are an environmentally friendly business.

SILENTNIGHT
www.silentnight.co.uk
The Eco Comfort collection of mattresses are made from recycled plastic bottles.

SMALLABLE
www.en.smallable.com
Stylish European home and living brands including Madam Stoltz, Communauté De Biens, Honest Skincare and Ferm Living.

SPAZA STORE
www.spazastore.com
Plastic-free kitchenware for the home, including dry goods bags and cotton dish covers produced by women working from home in impoverished communities in South Africa.

TRUTHBRUSH
www.thetruthbrush.com
Beautiful toothbrushes designed in Devon and made from organically farmed bamboo.

WEAVER GREEN
www.weavergreen.com
Beautiful, handwoven rugs and textiles made entirely from recycled plastic bottles.

WEEZ & MERL
www.weezandmerl.com
Marble-effect homewares made from recycled plastic.

ZERO WASTE CLUB
www.zero-waste-club.com
UK-based initiative offering plastic-free, zero-waste groceries plus body and skin care, bamboo straws and toothbrushes.

INSPIRING NATURAL LIVING INSTAGRAMMERS TO FOLLOW:
@finelittlegoods
@the_estate_trentham
@simply.living.well
@thesourcebulkfoods
@mothstyle
@captainsrest
@thebasicsstore
@generalstore
@packagefreeshop
@imperfectinteriors
@forestbound
@thenorrmans
@lindeborgsecoretreat
@meltdesignstudio
@lifelaeva
@plathuset
@mysuburbanfarm
@hostedbynature
@posyflowersandgifts

picture credits

1 Forest House in Sussex (available for hire through lightlocations.com); 2–3 Susannah and David le Mesurier's home in Wales; 4 The artisan studio of organic beauty brand LA-EVA; 5 An artists's house in the Netherlands; 6–7 Forest House in Sussex (available for hire through lightlocations.com); 8–9 Worton Organic Garden Oxfordshire, owned by David and Anneke Blake; 10–12 Lindeborgs Eco Retreat, designed and owned by Julia and Carl Lindeborg, lindeborgs.com; 13 left Forest House in Sussex (available for hire through lightlocations.com); 13 right Apifera, a stone cottage in Herefordshire available to rent through uniquehomestays.com; 14 An artists's house in the Netherlands; 15–17 The home of garden designer and author Dorthe Kvist meltdesignstudio. com; 18–19 Lindeborgs Eco Retreat, designed and owned by Julia and Carl Lindeborg, lindeborgs.com; 20 above left and centre Lindeborgs Eco Retreat, designed and owned by Julia and Carl Lindeborg, lindeborgs.com; 20 above right Susannah and David le Mesurier's home in Wales; 21 The Norrmans Boutique B&B, Denmark; 22 The artisan studio of organic beauty brand LA-EVA; 23 left Susannah and David le Mesurier's home in Wales; 23 right Lindeborgs Eco Retreat, designed and owned by Julia and Carl Lindeborg, lindeborgs.com; 24 above left Interior design by Beth Dadswell of imperfectinteriors.co.uk; 24 above right The Norrmans Boutique B&B, Denmark; 24 below left An artists's house in the Netherlands; 25–26 Susannah and David le Mesurier's home in Wales; 27 Forest House in Sussex (available for hire through lightlocations.com); 28 left Lindeborgs Eco Retreat, designed and owned by Julia and Carl Lindeborg, lindeborgs.com; 28 centre The home of garden designer and author Dorthe Kvist meltdesignstudio.com; 28 right The artisan studio of organic beauty brand LA-EVA; 29 An artists's house in the Netherlands; 30 The home of garden designer and author Dorthe Kvist meltdesignstudio.com; 31–32 The Norrmans Boutique B&B, Denmark; 33 left Interior design by Beth Dadswell of imperfectinteriors.co.uk; 33 right The home and garden of Wil and Bertus Aldershof-Koch, Smidse Voorstonden Bed & Breakfast; 34 left The artisan studio of organic beauty brand LA-EVA; 34 right and 35 Lindeborgs Eco Retreat, designed and owned by Julia and Carl Lindeborg, lindeborgs.com; 36 Susannah and David le Mesurier's home in Wales; 37 above left and below right The Norrmans Boutique B&B, Denmark; 37 above right Interior design by Beth Dadswell of imperfectinteriors.co.uk; 38 left The home of Debora Treep and Jan van Pelt in the Netherlands; 38 Lindeborgs Eco Retreat, designed and owned by Julia and Carl Lindeborg, lindeborgs.com; 38 right The home of garden designer and author Dorthe Kvist meltdesignstudio.com; 39 The artisan studio of organic beauty brand LA-EVA; 40 The Norrmans Boutique B&B, Denmark; 41 Susannah and David le Mesurier's home in Wales; 42 above left Susannah and David le Mesurier's home in Wales; 42 above right Lindeborgs Eco Retreat, designed and owned by Julia and Carl Lindeborg, lindeborgs.com; 42 below left and 43 Apifera, a stone cottage in Herefordshire available to rent through uniquehomestays. com; 44 The Norrmans Boutique B&B, Denmark; 45 above The artisan studio of organic beauty brand LA-EVA; 45 below Susannah and David le Mesurier's home in Wales; 46–47 Interior design by Beth Dadswell of imperfectinteriors.co.uk; 48 left Lindeborgs Eco Retreat, designed and owned by Julia and Carl Lindeborg, lindeborgs.com; 48 centre The home of Debora Treep and Jan van Pelt in the Netherlands; 48 right An artists's house in the Netherlands; 49 Interior design by Beth Dadswell of imperfectinteriors.co.uk; 50 left Lindeborgs Eco Retreat, designed and owned by Julia and Carl Lindeborg, lindeborgs.com; 50 right and 51 above left The home of garden designer and author Dorthe Kvist meltdesignstudio.com; 51 above right Susannah and David le Mesurier's home in Wales; 51 below An artists's house in the Netherlands; 52 The home of garden designer and author Dorthe Kvist meltdesignstudio. com; 53 Apifera, a stone cottage in Herefordshire available to rent through uniquehomestays.com; 54 above left and above right The home of Debora Treep and Jan van Pelt in the Netherlands; 54 below left Lindeborgs Eco Retreat, designed and owned by Julia and Carl Lindeborg, lindeborgs.com; 54 below right The home and garden of Wil and Bertus Aldershof-Koch, Smidse Voorstonden Bed & Breakfast; 55 An artists's house in the Netherlands; 56 Forest House in Sussex (available for hire through lightlocations.com); 57 The Norrmans Boutique B&B, Denmark; 58 Lindeborgs Eco Retreat, designed and owned by Julia and Carl Lindeborg, lindeborgs.com; 59 left The Norrmans Boutique B&B, Denmark; 59 centre Lindeborgs Eco Retreat, designed and owned by Julia and Carl Lindeborg, lindeborgs.com; 59 right The artisan studio of organic beauty brand LA-EVA; 60–61 Susannah and David le Mesurier's home in Wales; 62–63 Interior design by Beth Dadswell of imperfectinteriors.co.uk; 64 far left The Norrmans Boutique B&B, Denmark; 64–65 Interior design by Beth Dadswell of imperfectinteriors.co.uk; 66–69 An artists's house in the Netherlands; 70–71 The home of Debora Treep and Jan van Pelt in the Netherlands; 72–73 The home of garden designer and author Dorthe Kvist meltdesignstudio.com; 74–75 Lindeborgs Eco Retreat, designed and owned by Julia and Carl Lindeborg, lindeborgs.com; 76–77 Susannah and David le Mesurier's home in Wales; 78–79 Forest House in Sussex (available for hire through lightlocations.com); 80 above Susannah and David le Mesurier's home in Wales; 80 below Forest House in Sussex (available for hire through lightlocations.com); 81 Susannah and David le Mesurier's home in Wales; 82–83 An artists's house in the Netherlands; 84 and 85 above The home of garden designer and author Dorthe Kvist meltdesignstudio.com; 85 below Forest House in Sussex (available for hire through lightlocations.com); 86–89 Apifera, a stone cottage in Herefordshire available to rent through uniquehomestays.com; 90 above left Susannah and David le Mesurier's home in Wales; 90 above right and below left Forest House in Sussex (available for hire through lightlocations.com); 91 The home and garden of Wil and Bertus Aldershof-Koch, Smidse Voorstonden Bed & Breakfast; 92–93 The home of Debora Treep and Jan van Pelt in the Netherlands; 94–95 An artists's house in the Netherlands; 96 Interior design by Beth Dadswell of imperfectinteriors.co.uk; 97 The Norrmans Boutique B&B, Denmark; 98 above Forest House in Sussex (available for hire through lightlocations.com); 98 below left Interior design by Beth Dadswell of imperfectinteriors.co.uk; 99 The Norrmans Boutique B&B, Denmark; 100–101 Susannah and David le Mesurier's home in Wales; 102–103 An artists's house in the Netherlands; 104–105 The home of Debora Treep and Jan van Pelt in the Netherlands; 106 Apifera, a stone cottage in Herefordshire available to rent through uniquehomestays.com; 107 above The Norrmans Boutique B&B, Denmark; 107 below Forest House in Sussex (available for hire through lightlocations.com); 108 and 109 left Susannah and David le Mesurier's home in Wales; 109 right Forest House in Sussex (available for hire through lightlocations.com); 110–111 The home and garden of Wil and Bertus Aldershof-Koch, Smidse Voorstonden Bed & Breakfast; 112 Lindeborgs Eco Retreat, designed and owned by Julia and Carl Lindeborg, lindeborgs.com; 113 above The home and garden of Wil and Bertus Aldershof-Koch, Smidse

business credits

Voorstonden Bed & Breakfast; 113 below Lindeborgs Eco Retreat, designed and owned by Julia and Carl Lindeborg, lindeborgs.com; 114–115 Forest House in Sussex (available for hire through lightlocations.com); 116 and 117 left Interior design by Beth Dadswell of imperfectinteriors.co.uk; 117 right The home and garden of Wil and Bertus Aldershof-Koch, Smidse Voorstonden Bed & Breakfast; 118 Forest House in Sussex (available for hire through lightlocations.com); 119 left Apifera, a stone cottage in Herefordhsire available to rent through uniquehomestays.com; 119 right Forest House in Sussex (available for hire through lightlocations.com); 120 Apifera, a stone cottage in Herefordhsire available to rent through uniquehomestays.com; 121 The home of garden designer and author Dorthe Kvist meltdesignstudio.com; 122 Apifera, a stone cottage in Herefordshire available to rent through uniquehomestays.com; 123 Forest House in Sussex (available for hire through lightlocations.com); 124–127 Lindeborgs Eco Retreat, designed and owned by Julia and Carl Lindeborg, lindeborgs.com; 128–129 Interior design by Beth Dadswell of imperfectinteriors.co.uk; 130 left Susannah and David le Mesurier's home in Wales; 131 left The home of garden designer and author Dorthe Kvist meltdesignstudio.com; 131 right The home and garden of Wil and Bertus Aldershof-Koch, Smidse Voorstonden Bed & Breakfast; 132 The Norrmans Boutique B&B, Denmark; 133 Lindeborgs Eco Retreat, designed and owned by Julia and Carl Lindeborg, lindeborgs.com; 134–135 Worton Organic Garden Oxfordshire, owned by David and Anneke Blake; 136 The Norrmans Boutique B&B, Denmark; 137 The home of Debora Treep and Jan van Pelt in the Netherlands; 138 and 139 left Worton Organic Garden Oxfordshire, owned by David and Anneke Blake; 139 right The Norrmans Boutique B&B, Denmark; 140 left The Norrmans Boutique B&B, Denmark; 140 right and 141 Apifera, a stone cottage in Herefordhsire available to rent through uniquehomestays.com; 142 Worton Organic Garden Oxfordshire, owned by David and Anneke Blake; 143 left The artisan studio of organic beauty brand LA-EVA; 143 right Worton Organic Garden Oxfordshire, owned by David and Anneke Blake; 144 left Lindeborgs Eco Retreat, designed and owned by Julia and Carl Lindeborg, lindeborgs.com; 144 right Forest House in Sussex (available for hire through lightlocations.com); 145 above Worton Organic Garden Oxfordshire, owned by David and Anneke Blake; 145 below left The home of Debora Treep and Jan van Pelt in the Netherlands; 145 below right Forest House in Sussex (available for hire through lightlocations.com); 146 left Apifera, a stone cottage in Herefordshire available to rent through uniquehomestays.com; 146 right The home and garden of Wil and Bertus Aldershof-Koch, Smidse Voorstonden Bed and Breakfast; 147 above An artists's house in the Netherlands; 147 below Forest House in Sussex (available for hire through lightlocations.com); 148 left The Norrmans Boutique B&B, Denmark; 148 right Worton Organic Garden Oxfordshire, owned by David and Anneke Blake; 149 The home and garden of Wil and Bertus Aldershof-Koch, Smidse Voorstonden Bed & Breakfast; 150 and 151 above Worton Organic Garden Oxfordshire, owned by David and Anneke Blake; 151 below The artisan studio of organic beauty brand LA-EVA; 152 Forest House in Sussex (available for hire through lightlocations.com); 153 Susannah and David le Mesurier's home in Wales; 155 The artisan studio of organic beauty brand LA-EVA; 160 Apifera, a stone cottage in Herefordshire available to rent through uniquehomestays.com.

B&B SMIDSE VOORSTONDEN
smidse-voorstonden.nl
Pages 33 right, 54 below right, 91, 110–111, 117 right, 131 right, 146 right, 149.

DAVID AND ANNEKE BLAKE
Worton Organic Garden
Worton
Nr Cassington
Oxfordshire OX29 4SU
www.wortonorganicgarden.com
Pages 8–9, 134–135, 138, 139 left, 142, 143 right, 145 above, 148 right, 150, 151 above.

FOREST HOUSE
Location in Sussex
available for hire through
lightlocations.com
Pages 1, 6–7, 13 left, 27, 56, 78–79, 80 below, 85 below, 90 above right, 90 below left, 98 above, 107 below, 109 right, 114–115, 118, 119 right, 123, 144 right, 145 below right, 147 below, 152.

IMPERFECT INTERIORS
imperfectinteriors.co.uk
Pages 24 above, 33 left, 37 above right, 46–47, 49, 62–63, 64, 65, 96, 98 below left, 116, 117 left, 128, 129.

DORTHE KVIST
Melt Design Studio
Meltdesignstudio.com
Pages 15–17, 28 centre, 30, 38 right, 50 right, 51 above left, 52, 72–73, 84, 85 above, 121, 131 left.

LA-EVA
LA-EVA.com
Organic beauty brand.

Other artists and designers
to be credited:
Textiles Louisa Maybury Textiles
Picasso Prints Dantzig Gallery, Woodstock
Floral Crowns Nina Carrington
Chandelier and Mirrors Martha's Attic, Woodstock
Floral Displays Posy Flowers
Pages 4, 22, 28 right, 34 left, 39, 45 above, 59 right, 143 left, 151 below, 155.

LINDEBORGS ECO RETREAT
Eco farm stays, yoga
and retreats
www.lindeborgs.com
and also:
Architects
White Arkitekter
Magasinsgatan 10
403 17 Göteborg
Sweden
whitearkitekter.com
Pages 10–12, 18–19, 20 above left, 20 centre, 23 right, 28 left, 34 right, 35, 38 centre, 42 above right, 48 left, 50 left, 54 below left, 58, 59 centre, 74–75, 112, 113 below, 124–127, 133, 144 left.

ANNA AND LARS NORRMAN
The Norrmans Boutique B&B
IG: @thenorrmans
thenorrmans.com
Pages 21, 24 above right, 31, 32, 37 above left, 37 below right, 40, 44, 57, 59 left, 64 left, 97, 99, 107 above, 132, 136, 139 right, 140 left, 148 left.

UNIQUE HOME STAYS
uniquehomestays.com
13 right, 42 below left, 43, 53, 86–89, 106, 119 left, 120, 122, 140 right, 141, 146 left, 160.

index

Page numbers in italic refer to the illustrations

ACKNOWLEDGMENTS

It seems almost unbelievable that this is my ninth book to be published and, as ever, I would like to say a big thank you to my publishers for all the help and the hard work we put into producing this book together.

Thanks to a style theme that aims to tackle some of the issues our planet is currently facing, I have learned more and more about sustainability throughout the process of making this book, and I would like to thank all the people who have shared their eco-homes, barns, boutique B&Bs, organic gardens, studios and restoration projects with me. I have been so inspired by all your lovely natural designs and style ideas. It has been a complete pleasure to visit so many wonderful places and I would like to say a big thank you to Rachel Whiting for capturing them in all their glory with her stunning photography.

Finally thank you to my lovely family, and my husband Dave, who always support me. I love you.

P.S Please share your *Natural Living Style*, zero-waste and plastic-free ideas and eco-buys using the #naturallivingstyle hashtag on social media. I'd love to see your pics and ideas.